Math

KINGFISHER

NEW YORK

KINGFISHER
LONDON & NEW YORK

Published in the United States by Kingfisher,
175 Fifth Ave., New York, NY 10010
Kingfisher is an imprint of Macmillan Children's Books, London.
All rights reserved.

Consultant: Dr. Troy P. Regis

Designed and created by Basher
www.basherbooks.com
www.basherworld.com
www.bebo.com/simonbasher

Dedicated to David Coleman

Distributed in the U.S. by Macmillan, 175 Fifth Ave., New York, NY 10010
Distributed in Canada by H.B. Fenn and Company Ltd., 34 Nixon Road,
Bolton, Ontario L7E 1W2

Library of Congress Cataloging-in-Publication data has been applied for.

ISBN: 978-0-7534-6419-9

Kingfisher books are available for special promotions and premiums.
For details contact: Special Markets Department, Macmillan,
175 Fifth Ave., New York, NY 10010.

For more information, please visit www.kingfisherbooks.com

Printed in Taiwan
9 8 7 6 5 4 3 2 1
1TR/0410/UNT/SHENS/128MA/C

Note to readers: the website addresses listed above are correct at
the time of going to print. However, due to the ever-changing nature
of the Internet, website addresses and content can change. Websites
can contain links that are unsuitable for children. The publisher cannot
be held responsible for changes in website addresses or content or
for information obtained through a third party. We strongly advise
that Internet searches be supervised by an adult.

CONTENTS

Chapter 1
■ Number Bunch

Counting is one of the easiest things. One, two, three, four. And with ten handy counters at the end of your arms, getting to ten doesn't take much brainpower. But what are the Number Bunch for? Well, they're essential if you want to do math problems. They work in groups of tens. Ten tens becomes one hundred, ten hundreds becomes one thousand, and so on. So far so good, but math has a bad habit of getting harder. The Number Bunch is here to keep things from becoming befuddling and boring. When it comes to crunching numbers, they're the ones that count!

Zero

Infinity

Minus Numbers

Fraction

Decimal Fraction

Units

Zero
Number Bunch

✳ Youngster who has two lives—as a digit and as a number
✳ This digit allows you to imagine huge and tiny numbers
✳ It's also a tricky, mysterious number that equals nothing

I am El Zero, and I can dissolve you to nothing. You know my sign, the round mark of Zero. So be warned! I have extraordinary powers. Put my digit at the end of a number and I make the number ten times larger—leaping from 1 to 10 to 100 to 1,000 and so on forever. And then there's the curse of Zero. Divide by me and your calculator will return a big fat ERROR! Multiply by me and any number—no matter how large—vanishes, reduced to . . . well, Zero.

You see, I am something that stands for nothing. I am called nix, zip, zilch, nada, zippo . . . Hovering between being and not-being, I am one of the most important numbers in math. Yet I am so strange, so puzzling, that for hundreds of years even the smartest mathematicians in Europe didn't understand or use me.

Indian mathematicians first used Zero as a number 2,500 years ago.

● First book to include Zero written: A.D. 628
● Came to Europe via Muslim scholars
● The number Zero is an even number

Zero

∞Infinity
Number Bunch

* A mind-boggling customer that lies beyond all limits
* You cannot count or measure to Infinity or ever reach it
* Not a number, but closely involved with numbers

You'll never pin me down. I'm Infinity, beyond what you can even begin to imagine. Inconceivable! Okay, start counting: 1, 2, 3, 4, 5, 6 . . . And keep on counting: 7, 8, 9, 10, 11, 12 . . . And then count some more—and some more and some more. Hey, you say, this could go on forever. That's just the point! I exist, sure enough, and yet you will never reach me. I'm that endless road that teasingly keeps on disappearing off into the unknown.

Actually, I have a confession to make. Shh! Don't tell the others. I'm *not* a number—you can't use me to add or multiply or do the other things you do with numbers. But I'm so tied up with all of them that I feel fine about being here. By the way, my symbol is written like this: ∞. It's a closed double loop, sort of like a figure 8 taking a nap.

Georg Cantor (1845–1918) spent his life studying Infinity . . . and went crazy!

- Symbol name: lemniscate
- Symbol introduced by: John Wallis (1655)
- Medieval symbol: snake biting its tail

Infinity

Minus Numbers
Number Bunch

✳ These guys allow us to count lower than Zero
✳ A Minus Number is the inverse (opposite) of a positive one
✳ These negative numbers turn Add and Subtract on their heads

We are the beasts who live under the stairs. Count backward on the number scale: 7, 6, 5, 4, 3, 2, 1. It's like blastoff, isn't it? Then you reach the dark guardian of the gate, Zero. After that, you're with us, my friend, lurking in the dusty depths: −1, −2, −3, −4, −5, −6, −7 . . .

We're the opposites of the numbers you use to count real-life objects, such as apples, jellybeans, or your dad's gray hairs. Here, in the magical world of math, strange things happen. In the everyday world, you can't Subtract more than you have. You can't take nine cookies from a jar that has only five cookies in it, can you? But with us at your side, nothing could be easier. You're left with Minus Four cookies. Minus Four is the inverse of number four. If you add four to Minus Four, you get Zero.

Used to describe things like freezing temperatures—for example, −23°F.

● First known use: China (200s B.C.)
● First used by Arabs: A.D. 1000
● First used by Europeans: A.D. 1600s

Minus Numbers

Fraction

Number Bunch

※ Shadowy figure lurking in the gaps between whole numbers
※ Used to count the parts of a whole
※ The top figure is the numerator; the bottom is the denominator

I'm the broken bits and pieces. You can count whole pies on your fingers, but what if someone cuts a pie into four equal parts and eats a slice? That's where I come in—a not-quite-whole number. I look like this: $1/4$ or $2/3$, or even $1/600$. The bottom number says how many parts the whole is broken into—four in the case of $1/4$. The top says how many of those pieces you have—one.

Fraction

Fractions are used in stores to give discounts, such as $1/2$ price.

● First known use: China (c. 2800 B.C.)
● Proper Fractions: less than one (e.g., $5/7$)
● Improper Fractions: more than one (e.g., $9/7$)

Decimal Fraction

Number Bunch

* The same as Fraction, but shown in a different way
* Written as a figure or figures following a dot, or decimal point
* Points mark the end of whole numbers (147.5, 14.75, 1.475)

Decimal
Fraction

Okay, so I'm neat and orderly! Got a problem with that? Here's an example of my skills: 0.25. Scruffy old Fraction would call it ¹/₄. To get from Fraction to me, use your calculator to divide Fraction's top number by the bottom number. But I'm not always a tidy smarty-pants. Fraction's ¹/₃—one divided by three—becomes my 0.33333333. The threes recur (go on) into Infinity.

● First used by Arabs: A.D. 900s
● Digits on left of point: whole numbers
● Digits on right of point: Decimal Fractions

In some countries, people use a comma (,) for the decimal point.

Units
Number Bunch

☀ There is a world to measure, and this bunch does the measuring
☀ Divvy up all sorts, such as length, weight, temperature, time
☀ Their main coworkers are things like rulers and stopwatches

We are crack teams, highly trained, orderly, and ready for action. Our mission? To sort out the number world's measuring problems. How long is a football field? Call in our specialist yard Unit. How much soda is there in that big bottle? The liter squad are the guys for you. How heavy is the cat? Hooray! Here comes the pound brigade.

We can be part of the U.S. customary system or the metric system, and we come in all sizes. Inches (in. for short) and centimeters (cm) are useful for measuring small animals, such as hamsters. People, such as your big brother, are measured in feet (ft.) or meters (m). The metric Units conveniently form blocks of tens, hundreds, and thousands: 100 cm = 1 m, for example. The system that measures time divides into Units of 60 and 24.

The International System (SI), based on the metric system, is used in science.

● Number of seconds in a minute: 60
● Number of minutes in an hour: 60
● Number of hours in a day: 24

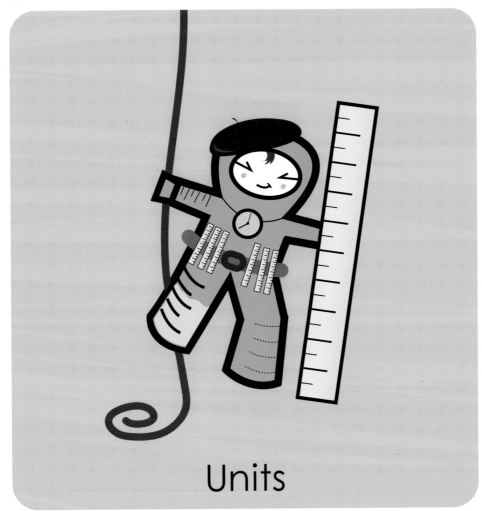

Units

Chapter 2
■ Special Sum-Things

You'll find this gang of number crunchers wherever you go. Get the hang of them and you're well into cracking the mysteries of numbers. The Special Sum-Things are ways of combining numbers, finding differences between them, sharing them, and zipping up and down the number scale with ease. They are mostly mental—not crazy—and just the sort of trick that you can do in your head. Using them can get you out of a tight spot. They will stick with you through thick and thin, and with them on your side, ain't nobody gonna make a fool outta you!

Add

Subtract

Multiply

Divide

χ

$+$ Add
Special Sum-Things

* With its big plus sign, this little fella joins numbers together
* The work it does is called addition
* In math, the total added together is called the sum

Out of all the Special Sum-Things, I'm the one who gives you more. Because I like putting bits and pieces together, numbers usually get bigger with me (the exception is when you Add a Minus Number to a positive number and get a smaller number: $3 + (-1) = 2$, for example).

I'm really simple to use—to Add numbers together, just stack one on top of another and count up each column separately, from right to left. You can use a calculator, an abacus, or your fingers and toes. And with me, you don't even have to do things in an orderly fashion: $27 + 35 + 8$ is the same as $35 + 8 + 27$, which is the same as $8 + 35 + 27$. They all Add up to 70. The only number that foxes me is Zero, because he makes no difference to any of my totals. Oh well!

HEAD PUZZLE You have 12 red jellybeans and 18 blue jellybeans. How many do you have in total? Try breaking the numbers up a little. $10 + 10 = 20$. Right? That's easy to do in your head. And $2 + 8 = 10$. So it's $20 + 10$, which equals 30. Hooray!

Add

Subtract
■ Special Sum-Things

- ✳ This unhappy character breaks numbers apart
- ✳ The work it does is called subtraction
- ✳ The total left over after subtraction is the difference

People often think I'm gloomy. Okay, I admit it, I'm the exact opposite of Add, that bubbly ball of smirking positivity. Because I'm always taking things away, numbers tend to get smaller with me around (the only exception is when you Subtract a bigger Minus Number from a smaller Minus Number and get a positive number: $(-3) - (-5) = 2$).

I have my uses, though, and some people like me. Ask any cupcake craver, fudge fiend, or jellybean junkie. With my long-dash minus sign, I'm their favorite, because the only way to enjoy cake is to Subtract a slice. But if you want your piece of cake, you have to mind your manners—I demand order. As you know, 5 pieces of cake minus 2 pieces is not the same as 2 pieces of cake minus 5 pieces (which is impossible in real life but possible in mathematics!)

HEAD PUZZLE You buy a bag of 49 gummi bears. Sally takes 14. How many do you have left? Try counting on. From 14 to 20 is 6. Easy! From 20 to 40 is 20. And then there's the last 9. $6 + 20 + 9 = 35$. So $49 - 14 = 35$. Get it?

Subtract

✕ Multiply
■ Special Sum-Things

☀ A greedy guzzler who hoards numbers together
☀ This big guy's work is called multiplication
☀ In math, the total provided by multiplication is the product

When I'm around, whole numbers get much bigger much faster than with that tiresome Add. That's because I gather up whole groups of numbers rather than just single units. Three times four means three helpings of four, which gives you much more than three plus four (12 rather than 7). My sign is x, the sign of the times! Memorize your times tables and I'll make you rich.

I do have one thing in common with Add—neither of us is worried about order. Two sets of number 3 is the same as three sets of number 2. The number 1 cramps my style a little. Multiply any number by 1 and you get the same old number you started with—one set of number 11 is plain and simple 11. As for Zero . . . use me to Multiply by Zero and you get nothing. Zero sets of number 5 is always zilch.

HEAD PUZZLE Tom gives you a bunch of four marigolds. All marigolds have 13 petals. How many petals are there in the bunch? Well, 4 = 2 x 2, so the bunch has 2 x 2 x 13 petals. That's better! 2 x 2 x 13 = 2 x 26 = 52.

Multiply

÷ Divide
■ Special Sum-Things

※ An equal-minded pirate who portions out numbers fairly
※ This even-steven's work is called division
※ In math, the number being divvied up is called the dividend

I'm Multiply's opposite, here to split up the loot and make sure everyone gets equal portions of the pie. If there's one of you, you can have the stash all to yourself, but if there's more than one, you need me. You'll find me to be an evenhanded sort of fella, one who always does the carving up fairly. But one thing's for sure—dividing by a whole number makes the total number go down. In other words, each portion I give is smaller than the total amount. You have to use Multiply to get back to where you started.

Sometimes, I can't slice things up into neat round numbers. So, in my quest for fairness, I use underworld connections and create Fractions—shady, not-quite-whole numbers that make the arithmetic work. My sign is ÷, the division sign, which also has the fancy Greek name *obelus*.

HEAD PUZZLE You, Jane, and Andy are going to buy a toy that costs $12.21. How much does each of you have to chip in? Hey! That's why you learn your times tables. 3 x 4 = 12. Yes? And 3 x 7 = 21. So each owes $4 and 7¢. Or $4.07.

÷

Divide

X

◼ Special Sum-Things

✴ A nameless secret agent who haunts math equations
✴ This "x"-citing creature has been operating for over 1,800 years
✴ Used in algebra to help you figure out unknown quantities

I am the faceless one. With my secret code name "x" I lurk in the shadows of the Special Sum-Things gang. I am what's called a variable—a symbol put in place of an unknown, mystery quantity. I am "x"-tremely useful and not just to friendly old mathematicians.

Let me "x"-plain. Say that you and Angus buy a bag of candy. You both eat two pieces, and Angus hides four more in his pocket. If you bought 10 pieces, how many are left in the candy bag? 2 pieces + 2 pieces + 4 pieces + x (unknown number of pieces left in the bag) = 10. With me to help, you don't have to look in the bag. Instead, figure it out on your fingers that x = 2. That means Angus took most of the remaining goodies! See? I have the x-factor! Goodness me, all this punning is "x"-hausting!

HEAD PUZZLE Stay calm! Think straight! Your marbles have scattered all over the place. Amy's found 11. Pete's found 8. You had 24 in all. Okay, 11 + 8 + x (the number missing) = 24. 11 + 8 = 19. Subtract that from 24. You still have 5 to find.

χ

Chapter 3
■ Shape Shifters

Slippery! Slidy! These are the Shape Shifters, the building blocks of everything you see around you. Math has them and their shifty ways down to a fine art—it's called geometry. Where two straight Lines meet, you get an Angle. Three straight Lines and three Angles make a Triangle. This is magic! A square has equal length and width, right? Give it depth as well and it can become a cube. In the world of geometric shapes, you move through dimensions, from 1-D to 2-D to 3-D. This is the best building set you'll ever have. Enjoy!

Line

Angle

Circle

Pi

Triangle

Quadrilaterals

Polygon

3-D Shapes

Area

Volume

Line
▪ Shape-Shifters

✳ A simple character who lives in 1-D only
✳ In geometry, a Line has length but no width
✳ Lines are said to intersect when they meet or cross one another

I'm the simplest shape there is. Think of me as the skinniest beanpole you ever came across. There's only length in 1-D—that's all. A Line is neither 2-D nor 3-D. The other Shape Shifters look down on me for my uncluttered lifestyle, but let me tell you one thing: not one of them can be drawn without me.

When I take the shortest route between two points—as the crow flies—I'm a straight Line. When I curve elegantly, I'm an arc. And here's another fact—I'm infinite. When you see a Line with two ends, it's only a part (or segment) of me. Sometimes I intersect with another Line, forming an Angle. Sometimes I run parallel with another Line. So, like train tracks, my parallel Line and I never move away from each other, and we never move any closer.

Greek mathematician Euclid wrote about Lines and geometry, c. 300 B.C.

● Perpendicular Lines cross at right Angles
● Parallel Lines always run side by side
● Chord: a Line segment linking two points on a circle

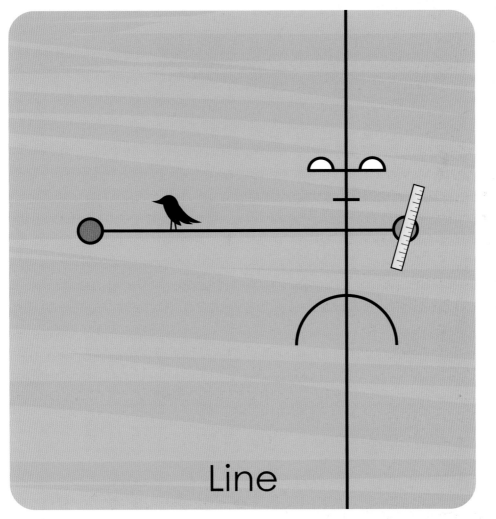

Line

Angle

▪ Shape Shifters

* ✳ A sharp customer, found where two Lines meet
* ✳ Measured using degrees, often written as a small circle: 60°
* ✳ You use a protractor to measure Angles

No angel, I'm a big cheese face who has many moods. Sometimes I'm just right. Other times, I can be acute, obtuse, or reflex. Okay, down to business. Imagine two straight Lines on a page. Unless they're parallel, their paths will cross, and that's where you'll meet me. If you imagine turning one of the Lines so that it sits snugly on top of the other, I'm the amount you have to crank it around.

If you're a skateboarder, we're already buddies. Mastered the 360? Well, 360 is short for 360°—a full or complete turn. What about a neat quarter turn? That's 90°. A 90° Angle is a right Angle—right, proper, and exact. Acute Angles are less than 90°—sharp and not so sweet. Then you get the obtuse Angles that blunder along between 90° and 180°. Any Angle bigger than 180° is a reflex Angle.

In geometry, Angles are shown by a small arc between two Lines.

* ● Whole turn (Circle): 360°
* ● Half turn (straight Line): 180°
* ● Quarter turn (right Angle): 90°

Angle

Circle

Shape Shifters

* Perfectly rounded, this character is a real roller
* All parts of its edge are the same distance from its center
* You need a compass to draw a perfectly round Circle

I'm a chubby-cheeked bundle of fun. Every time you draw a happy face, chances are it's beaming out of me. And of course anytime you hop on your bike and pedal down the street or do a wheelie, you're using my cool talent for spinning, or rotating. Yes, I get things rolling. It's a knack I owe to one simple fact—all points on my perimeter (the outside line that forms my shape) are an equal distance from my center.

I'm so one of a kind that my vital statistics have their own special names. My width is called my diameter (*d*). The distance from my center to my perimeter is my radius (*r*)—half my diameter. The length of my perimeter is that noble fella circumference (*C*)—"Sir Cumference." To measure my Area (*A*), you'll need the help of my friend Pi (π).

In ancient times, many people believed that the Circle was divine.

* Diameter: $d = 2 \times r$
* Circumference: $C = \pi \times d$
* Area: $A = \pi \times r \times r$

Circle

π Pi

Shape Shifters

✳ A mysterious number with many math tricks up its sleeve
✳ Defined as the Ratio of a Circle's circumference to its diameter
✳ Often written as the Greek letter π, pronounced "pie"

As simple as Pi? Hmm! Up to a point. Mathematicians love me—I'm their favorite dish (pie, get it?). But I take a bit of getting used to. How do you find me? Take Circle's circumference and Divide that by the diameter. It doesn't matter how large or small the Circle is, the number you get will always be the same—me, Pi!

Crazy, isn't it? And they do call me an irrational number, which could mean that I'm a bit wacky. But I'm sane, really. It's just that you can't capture me neatly in a Fraction. So what is my magic number? 3.14159 . . . and on and on and on. The number never ends and never repeats. Spooky! And don't think I'm just some funny little oddity. No, I'm key. For example, you need me to figure out the Area of a Circle. And that's just one of my tricks.

Pi to 20 decimal places:
3.14159265358979323846

● $\pi = C \div d$
● π: first letter of Greek word for perimeter
● Surface Area of a sphere: $4 \times \pi \times r \times r$

Pi

Triangle
Shape Shifters

* Three corners and three straight sides—that's a Triangle
* There are four different kinds of Triangles
* A Triangle's three interior (inside) Angles add up to 180°

"Tri" pushing me around, big fella, and I'll knock you into a three-cornered hat. I'm rigid! Three means strength, and you'll need a sledgehammer to shift my shape. I do have different forms, though. Come meet them!

Prettiest first! Meet the equilaterals—all three sides the same length, with three dainty 60° Angles. Next, the isosceles—two sides the same, two equal Angles. Uh-oh! Here come the scalenes—no sides or Angles the same. Last, the right Triangles, with one 90° corner. These dudes hook up with a famous rule, the Pythagorean theorem: "The squaw on the hippopotamus equals the sum of the squaws on the other two hides." Just kidding! "The square of the hypotenuse equals the sum of the squares of the other two sides."

If "c" stands for hypotenuse, Pythagoras's equation is $a^2 + b^2 = c^2$.

● Area: $1/2$ x length of base x height
● Right Triangle's longest side: hypotenuse
● Right Triangle's other sides: legs, or catheti

Triangle

Quadrilaterals
Shape Shifters

* These boxy characters all have four straight sides
* They include squares, rectangles, and many more
* The name comes from Latin words meaning "four sides"

Sharp edged and orderly, we march to a strict rule of four—four corners, four straight sides. Squares are special Quads, neatly presented with four 90° Angles at their corners and four equal sides. But don't think we're just a bunch of old squares—we come in all kinds of shapes.

Rectangles let two of their sides grow longer but keep their corners at a 90° Angle. Rhombuses (like wacky squares) and parallelograms (like wacky rectangles) live life on the slant. They let their corners slide off the right Angle, although their two pairs of opposite sides are still parallel. Tricky trapezoids only bother to keep one pair of parallel sides, while kites (shaped like the ones you fly) have no parallel sides at all. Kites, however, are symmetrical—one half mirrors the other half.

The geometrical kite was named after the shape of flying kites.

* All Quadrilaterals have four sides
* All Quadrilaterals have four corners
* Interior Angles add up to 360°

Quadrilaterals

Polygon
Shape Shifters

* The royal ruler of the 2-D flatlands
* Includes all geometrical shapes with straight sides
* The name comes from Greek words meaning "many Angles"

I'm the queen of diamonds (the four-sided ones in packs of cards) and many more. But before I start boasting about my loyal subjects, let's count to ten in Greek—don't worry, I know what I'm doing. Here goes: *ena* (one), *dio* (two), *tria* (three), *tessera* (four), *pente* (five), *hexi* (six), *hepta* (seven), *octo* (eight), *ennea* (nine), *deca* (ten).

Excellent! Well, you've already met my trusty Triangles (*tria*, three, see?) and my worthy Quadrilaterals. Here are some of the others: my pentagons (five-sided shapes), hexagons (six-sided), heptagons (seven-sided), octagons (eight-sided), and so on. Some are regular, with equal sides and Angles. Some are highly irregular—their sides are a jumble of lengths and their corners a ragbag of Angles. But they are all mine, all Polygons.

A Polygon with a million sides is called a megagon.

* Nonagon (or enneagon): nine sides
* Decagon: ten sides
* Hendecagon: 11 sides

Polygon

3-D Shapes
▪ Shape Shifters

☀ The 3-D top dogs of the Shape Shifter gang
☀ They live in the same 3-D world we all live in
☀ 3-D Shapes have depth (or height), as well as length and width

We're space cadets. We fill space. Think of that poor Line, with length but no width or depth. Or even the Polygon crew with length and width, but still no depth. With us, you get all three—length, width, and depth. Cubes, spheres, cones, and pyramids, that's us—objects you can sit on, store things in, or kick around a park.

There's a lot that's special about us 3-D guys. Each of us fills up a certain space, called its Volume. Our surfaces, like skins stretched over us, have Area. In geometry, each of our sides is called a face. Our faces meet along edges that come together in pointy corners. Each corner is called a vertex, from an old Latin word meaning "top," like the spiky top of a mountain. Our oddball is the sphere, which has only one face—no edges and no vertices.

3-D objects with flat faces and straight edges are polyhedrons.

● Cube: boxy shape with six square faces
● Sphere: round like a billiard ball
● Cone: round base, pointed tip

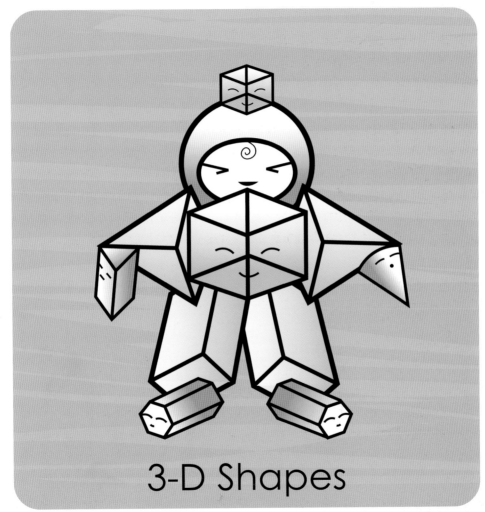

3-D Shapes

Area
Shape Shifters

- Nerdy but handy, this character sizes up 2-D space
- The size of any surface, flat or rounded, is its Area
- Measured in square Units, such as square feet (sq. ft.)

I'm like a piece of cloth rolled out over something—the top of your kitchen table, for example. The amount of 2-D space I cover is the thing's surface Area. Some call me flat and boring, but they're just plain wrong. Every surface has its Area, and that includes the surface of your basketball. Nobody can call that flat and boring.

All right! Let's get to work. Grab a box of chocolate! How big is the top of the box? Okay, measure how long the top is—9 in., say. Then measure how wide it is—8 in. Multiply one by the other—9 x 8—and that's me: 72. The top of your box has a surface Area of 72 sq. in. Easy, wasn't it? Do the same thing with the box's other five faces, then Add all your results together. You now have the box's total surface Area—top, bottom, sides, and all.

Land area is often measured using acres or hectares.

- 1 hectare = 107,639 sq. ft. (10,000 m²)
- 1 acre = 43,560 sq. ft. (almost 4,047 m²)
- Area of U.S.: 3,794,100 sq. mi. (9,826,675 km²)

Area

Volume
▦ Shape Shifters

※ A funky rocker used to measure 3-D space
※ The amount of 3-D space a thing takes up is its Volume
※ Measured in cubic Units, such as cubic feet (cu. ft.)

"Turn up the Volume, baby." When you think of me, that's what you imagine, isn't it? Loud music and big rock-star hair. Well, I have other skills. I can tell you the size of a 3-D object—that kind of Volume. Even better, I work hand in hand with capacity—how much of something another object will hold. Now, that can be truly vital information, like how much soda a bottle contains.

Remember Area's box of chocolate? It was 9 in. long and 8 in. wide. Let's say it was 3 in. deep. What's its Volume? Easy! Multiply the three numbers together and you get me: 9 in. x 8 in. x 3 in. = 216 cu. in. For rounded things like bottles, you'll have to get in touch with Pi. Always happy to lend a hand, Pi will help you calculate the Volumes of cylinders, cones, spheres, and other curvy 3-D Shapes.

Capacity is usually measured in Units such as quarts or liters.

● Volume of a cube: a^3 (a = length)
● Volume of a cylinder: height (h) x π x r^2
● Volume of a cone: $^1/_3$ x h x π x r^2

Volume

Chapter 4
Data Gang

Hot stuff, this bunch! Data is information—key statistics, such as how tall you've grown over the past few months or how many points your favorite basketball players have scored. But what's the point of this stuff if you don't do something with it? The Data Gang will show you how. Turn those points into a kind of picture (or graphic)—a multicolored Bar Graph where you can see at a glance who's scored the most. Draw a Line Graph showing how fast you've grown! Figure out some Averages! Calculate percentages! You'll be so busy, you won't know where the time has gone.

Average

Ratio

Percent

Bar Graph

Pie Chart

Line Graph

Average
■ Data Gang

☀ There's nothing ordinary about this Average Joe
☀ Its special skills are finding midpoints among numbers
☀ Has three forms: the mode, the median, and the mean

It's Captain Average to you. My name may be Average, but there is nothing ordinary or "plain vanilla" about me. Yes, I drive down the middle of the road so no one can pass me. But that's my job—figuring out the exact midway point among a set of two or more numbers.

Take my "mean" trick. Your aunt Mary—every time you visit her, she gives you a bag of candy, bless her! Last time, the bag had 19 pieces in it. The time before, it had 16 pieces, and the time before that, seven. What's the Average (or mean) number of pieces she's given you per visit? Add up the total number of pieces: 19 + 16 + 7 = 42. Divide your total by the number of visits: 42 ÷ 3 = 14. Over three visits, she's given you an Average of 14 pieces per visit. Not bad, really. She's not mean!

The Greek letter μ (mu) is sometimes used for the mean.

● Mean: Average of a set of numbers
● Mode: most common number in a set
● Median: the middle value in a set

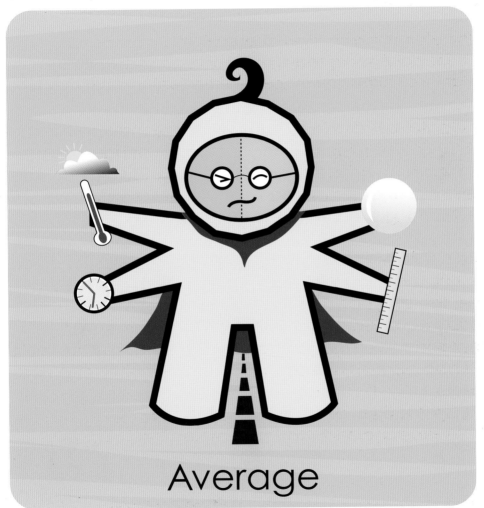

Average

Ratio
Data Gang

* This tidy character loves to keep things in proportion
* Shows how much there is of one thing compared with another
* Written as numbers with a colon between them, such as 4:1

Okay, let's cut to the chase! You have five marbles in your hand. Two are red, and three are blue. The Ratio of red marbles to blue ones is two to three—that's 2:3. You can also use me for the odds (or chances) of something happening. If you flip a coin, there are two possible results, both equally likely: heads or tails. The odds of getting heads or tails are 1:1.

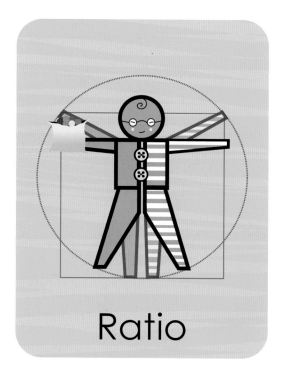

Ratio

Map scales use Ratio, e.g. 1:5,000 (in life, everything is 5,000 times bigger).

* First known use: 1000 B.C.
* Can be written as a Fraction: e.g. $2/3$
* Order is important: 5:2 is not 2:5

Percent %
Data Gang ▪

- ✷ A pinstriped slicker whose name means "per hundred"
- ✷ A kind of Fraction, based on parts of a hundred
- ✷ Can be written using its special % symbol: 40%, 75%, 100%

Percent

I keep track of things, like your score on a quiz. There were 20 questions and—genius that you are—you got 17 right. What's that as a percentage? Divide 17 by 20 and you get 0.85. Multiply that by 100 and you get 85. That is your score: 85%. Your brother did a quiz with 50 questions and got 38 right. Who did better? Answer: you did—he got only 76% right.

- ● 25% of something is one-fourth of it
- ● 50% of something is half of it
- ● 75% of something is three-fourths of it

Banks use percentages when people borrow money from them.

Bar Graph

■ Data Gang

✷ Smart and brightly colored, a graph that puts data into bars
✷ Good for data having to do with how often or how many
✷ Also good for preferences, such as people's favorite bands

In my fancy uniform, I'm off the charts for showing data in graphic (picture-like) form. I'm best when you want to compare things like results. Say that so far this season, Fred has scored six goals for the soccer team, Tony has kicked four, and you've scored two. I'll turn that into a graph, where Fred's bar is the highest, Tony's is a little shorter, and your bar is the lowest.

Bar Graph

Statistical Bar Graphs that display ranges of data are called histograms.

● Invented by William Playfair (1786)
● Bars can be vertical (upright)
● Bars can be horizontal (left to right)

Pie Chart
Data Gang

* A pie maker who shares fairly but not equally
* Shows data as Angles within a Circle
* The biggest scorer of anything gets the largest slice

Pie Chart

I offer the tastiest treats if you need wedges of data. When I divide a Circle into different-size slices—actually, Angles—you'll see at a glance who the big cheeses are. Let's grab those goal results from Bar Graph. Give the tallies to me and you'll see that out of 12 goals scored so far this season, Fred has scored half, Tony a third, and you . . . well, never mind!

● Pie Charts are divided into segments
● Calculate Fred's Angle: $6/12 \times 360 = 180°$
● Tony's Angle: $4/12 \times 360 = 120°$

The nurse Florence Nightingale used Pie Charts in the 1850s.

Line Graph
▪Data Gang

- ☀ A smooth customer who plays connect the dots with data
- ☀ Best for the kind of data that changes over time
- ☀ Has a horizontal x-axis and a vertical y-axis

Plotting and planning, I'm the secret agent of the Data Gang. But when I show you my results, everything's out in the open. My top-notch skill is for things that change over time—like your height over the past six months. First, you'll have to become a plotter like me. Draw your axes—said "ax-eez," not the "ax-iz" you use to chop wood—and label them neatly. The x-axis runs left to right along the bottom, and the y-axis runs upward on the left.

Put time along the x-axis—from 0 to 6 if you're plotting (showing) how much you've grown over six months. The y-axis is for the other set of data—your height. Put a dot or cross for how tall you were at the start of the six months, how tall you were after one month, after two months, and so on. Join the dots with lines, and there's your graph.

A pair of numbers called coordinates show a position on a Line Graph.

- ● Coordinates are written like this: (2,5)
- ● First number: position on x-axis
- ● Second number: position on y-axis

Line Graph

Index

O
obtuse Angle 32

P
parallel Lines 30
parallelogram 40, 63
pentagon 42
Percent (%) **55**
perimeter 34, 36, 63
Pi (π) 34, **36**, 48
Pie Chart **57**
Polygon **42**
polyhedron 44
prime number 64
protractor 32
pyramid 44, 64
Pythagorean theorem 38, 64

Q
Quadrilaterals **40**, 42, 63

R
radius 34, 36
Ratio 36, **54**
rectangle 40
reflex Angle 32
rhombus 40
right Angle 32
right Triangle 38

S
scalene Triangle 38
segment 30, 57
shapes
  1-D 28, 30
  2-D 28, 30, 34, 38, 40, 42,
    46, 63, 64
  3-D Shapes 28, 30, 44,
    48, 62–64
SI Units 14, 64
sphere 36, 44, 48
square 40
Subtract **20**
symmetry 40, 64

T
trapezoid 40
Triangle 28, **38**, 42

UV
Units **14**
vertex 44, 64
Volume 44, **48**

XYZ
χ **26**
x-axis 58, 62
y-axis 58, 62
Zero **6**, 10, 22

Glossary

Abacus A counting frame with horizontal rows of beads.

Algebra A branch of math that uses symbols and letters to represent unknown amounts.

Arc Part of the circumference of a circle, or a section of a curving line.

Average see **Mean**.

Axis (pl. **Axes**) On a graph, the two reference lines: the horizontal (for the x coordinate) and the vertical (for the y coordinate). The axis is also the "mirror image" line in symmetry—the midway line that divides a symmetrical object into two halves.

Capacity The amount that something can hold. Another word for volume.

Coordinates A pair of numbers (or letters) that are used to give positions on graphs and maps. They mark the point where a vertical line on the x-axis meets a horizontal line on the y-axis.

Difference The amount left over after subtracting one number from another—the difference between two numbers.

Digit A symbol used to make numerals. There are ten digits: 1, 2, 3, 4, 5, 6, 7, 8, 9, and 0. For example, the digits 1, 7, and 4 make the numeral 174.

Dozen A set of twelve.

Edge A line where two faces of a 3-D shape meet. For example, a cube has 12 edges.

Estimate A rough calculation.

Even number A number that can be divided by two—even numbers end with 2, 4, 6, 8, or 0.

Face A flat side of a 3-D shape. For example, a cube has six faces.

Factor Any number that can divide the number being divided (the dividend) without leaving a remainder.

Formula A mathematical rule written using symbols.

Geometry A branch of math that deals with shapes.

Inverse A term that means "opposite" in math: subtraction is the inverse of addition.

Mean The arithmetic average. To calculate the mean, add up all the amounts in a collection of data and divide the total by the number of amounts: $(50 + 25 + 25 + 45 + 55) \div 5 = 40$.

Median The number in the middle of an ordered set of numbers. If the set is 25, 25, 45, 50, and 55, the median is 45.

Metric system A system of measurement based on multiples of ten (tens, hundreds, thousands, and so forth).

Mode The number that occurs most often in a set of numbers. If the set is 50, 25, 25, 45, and 55, the mode is 25.

Odd number A number that cannot be divided by two—odd numbers end with 1, 3, 5, 7, or 9.

Parallelogram A quadrilateral with two pairs of equal-length, parallel sides and equal opposite angles.

Perimeter The distance around the outside of a 2-D shape.

Glossary

Perpendicular Lines that meet each other at right angles.

Prime number A number that can be divided only by itself and 1, such as 5, 7, 11, and 13. 1 is not a prime number.

Pyramid A 3-D shape with either a triangular base and three triangular faces or a square base and four triangular faces.

Pythagorean theorem Named after the Greek mathematician Pythagoras (c. 580 B.C.–c. 500 B.C.). He came up with a formula to solve the length of a right triangle's hypotenuse (the longest side): $a^2 + b^2 = c^2$.

SI The International System of Units—a metric system useful in math and science—based on seven defined units, including kilogram (weight), meter (length), and second (time).

Sum The result from adding numbers.

Symmetry A property of a 2-D or 3-D shape that can be reflected or rotated to "match" or fit with itself in another orientation. For example, the letter "A" has one line of symmetry, and an equilateral triangle has three.

Transformation To change a shape in one of three ways: flip (reflect), slide (translate), or turn (rotate).

U.S. customary system A system of measurement derived from units historically used in Great Britain, such as the foot.

Vertex (pl. **Vertices**) A corner of a 3-D shape. For example, a cube has eight vertices.

Whole number A number that you can use to count—somewhere from zero to infinity.